# Unsongs
# Volume 1.

by

Gabriel Hart

Close To The Bone Publishing

# Acknowledgments

Special thanks to Craig Douglas, Stephen J. Golds, B. F. Jones, Kev, and Chris at Close To The Bone and to all in the First Cut Poetry Collective.

*Dedicated to Rich Soos and Cholla needles, where some of these poems were originally published.*

# Contents

# Introduction

This is a book of poems.

While I'm known more as a songwriter, I feel the poem and the song have grown apart as two explicitly different entities – a de-evolution of culture when they should have stayed one and the same thing. So unless you're Dante Aliano-White or Charlotte McCaslin – two of the greatest living *poetic* songwriters I know of – this is our unfortunate reality.

Songs, as we know them today, have become what I prefer to call 'ego-jingles'. A singer's precious little summation of their soul they've sociopathically manipulated a small group into fleshing out then repeating, over and over, for little to no pay. Like a nightmare on a loop, how is this not a distinct vision of Hell? These days, like it or not, a song's sole purpose is to reduce itself into a commodity to sell albums for a label or alcohol for a club. Then, if enough money exists or has been raised behind your 'team', you are then lavished with praise from the press to then help sell ads in print magazines and online sites – or if you're really lucky, your song will appear in a car commercial to help the corporation appear more in tune with today's ever souring zeitgeist.

Poetry, on the other hand, is the lonely, thankless road – even when the poem is exceptional. But poetry is the true emergency, the means to an end, the cry for help, the declaration of independence, the scream in the forest that makes no sound, meant to be savored in the lightning strike moment of the poet's live reading or in reflective repose from their book.

So with the urging of Stephen J. Golds, I've culled 30 poetic forms never set to music because they were never meant to distract you. It was your choice to pick up this chapbook – it didn't assault

1

your eardrums when you were focusing on another task. Maybe one day I'll get around to compiling my own lyrics, but for now all you get are these *unsongs* in your hard-earned silence, assuming you don't suffer from tinnitus in taunting agony like I do.


Gabriel Hart

Morongo Valley, CA

January, 2021

# Rising

Born again
As a demon
In their own image
A lineage
Steeped in tradition
Banished to darkness
Their own shadows
Down here
I
Light the fires
From my earned
Erudition

I've been tied to fishing line
So they may dictate
My ascension
Yet my boiling blood
Makes a fuse of their impotence
As sparks burn up the binds
I am free of condescension

There I rise, with each light
These autonomous lanterns
Of true divinity
A demon's work
Never done
Yet, now in flight
To encounter

Every holder
Of my infinity

Only once did I look back
Anticipating
Flaps of my wings
But they retract
My rising
Propelled only
From my guttural
Growling

Every opponent, on a perch
Like figurines of arrogance
On display
As I moved through each
Insignificance
Their mouths
Wide open
With nothing to say

Confirmation, untouchable
Transparency looming
The sun expanded
As the exits
Every gatekeeper of layer
And in-fighting naysayer
Convoluted, proving
They no longer exist

Now, see my silhouette
Against that ball of fire
Your Hell below?
Merely my chrysalis
Your business?
My pleasure
To be this Demon
Anything to be
Your anti-thesis

# They Call Me Candle

...cause the night I finally saw twenty-one
Was the night I lost control of all of 'em
Candles
I was sure we were just having fun
'Till they all blurred into one single one
Candle
Here I stand
A hothead
Yet quiet as a smothered clue
Keeping constant vigil
Not just for everything we done
But for everything we gonna do

I stood erect
When I felt a warmth
From what I thought was
My fateful twin
But every time
She would meltdown
I'd see her wick
All ready
Charred
All the way down
Within
A pre-existing condition
She refused to
Handle

I'll keep my core
Hungry
Pale
Soft
Maintain my top
Red
Hot
Meltdown
In Balanced
Steady
Drops
Into a foundation
On
Lock

So if you try to knock me down
I'll only burn
This goddamn town
To the ground
Then, they will surely call me…

# Late Bloomer (With A Love Supreme)

I waited years for the coal train
I was feeling cold and mean
No more room
On the warm passenger train
I didn't give anybody anything
What in the world was I protecting?
Holding both hands over my heart
Choking it till began exploding
I could have sworn that I kept getting shot

And when that coal train finally came
It was hot to the touch
Before it burst into flames

I was a late bloomer with a love supreme
Endlessly brooding
Leaving scorched earth behind me
The more I got away with
The less epiphany

We met on a whiplash overcast day
When that sad junkie icon went blue
We didn't really have much at all to say
Both our hands in his same cookie jar, too
It felt like Earth had fallen off its axis
Distancing itself from its own moon
You and I clearly on different planets
So cruel
Similar orbits
But too soon

When I heard the horn then, I just plugged my ears
And I wouldn't see her again for the next twenty years

A late bloomer with a love supreme
I listened to the horn
Like it was the end of the world
Another late bloomer with a love supreme
My idea of letting go?
Retreating into my shadow

I did the splits over a fool's history
I punched a guitar as if it was my mind
I kissed every single face that would let me
While imagining the perfect kind
I caught myself pissing in my own cauldron
When I heard a sound that made me cry
I felt like something was about to happen
But I couldn't stop
Closing my eyes

# Abbreviated Alibi

His fingers crowd my mouth
Rubber glove olfactory gag
Asphyxiate, a reflex
My mouth, his magic hat
For his next trick
He pulls out my lie
"Do you smoke?"
I say nope
The abbreviated alibi

What should I have told him?
That smoke is my only time with God
Where I speak out loud
Take pause
To give thanks
Reflect proud
That I can't show gratitude
Unless I take my own self down a notch
Knowing every drag I take
Shaves a second of my life off?

That I must get to that "in-between"
In order to commune
And reconvene
With all the dead and the divine
As I blow the smoke up
Heavens high

That it all started when I was twelve and I missed my Aunt
I creaked open her old Volvo
Interior sun-cracked
The dead air escaped like a catacomb well-preserved
Helen!
Long gone but a part of her still there, though inert
Her cigarettes in the glove compartment
As I thought
"One won't hurt."

Teenage initiation
Into the decayed sublime
A lighter in her old pack
I lit the end in second's time
As if it were pre-destined
As if we were conversing
Through the puff of smoke
That made her gone
Now, she's universing!!!

Yes, I smoke for the divine and dead
Only on rare occasion
Each one with nuance, no regret
But with respect to their annihilation
Like that time under the black light
When we were not of sound mind
We stared into our embers
Exposed a world unkind
A tiny depiction of Hell
A Bosch painting come to life
A tale of overindulgence
Imbalance
Remembered

The dentist calls me mister
Three times
To make sure I'm still alive
I apologize
"Yes, I am."
I'll never tell another lie

# Conspiracy In Your Eyes

Two spiral staircases I'm careening down
Your eye sockets
I'm clawing to the bottom of
A stare that goes nowhere
Yet makes my stomach drop
Down a thousand stories
Aimed straight for my gut

And what a perfect time!
All my insides past their prime
Atmosphere so thick
Yet it's clear
For once
Outside
I wish I could say
The same
For your mind

There is a heavy weight in the air tonight
From the vast conspiracy in your eyes

I used to know you like I knew every hole in the wall
But I'm a man
I'm not a mouse
And you're a cryptic baby doll
Your image starts to fade
You're an eternal silhouette
And nothing is revealed
Besides your eyes
Becoming wet

My mouth is so dry
But I'm not thirsty for a lie
If only tears could leak *inside*
But you just can't make this cold statue cry

# Deep Root Delusion

To them, we are dreaming
Chatter teeth to the gums
Break the skin
Hit more bone
Screams erupt from our lungs

We will get kind of dizzy
Staring across the gap
But if we keep our heads spinning
The edges overlap

I fixate on the farthest
I haunt on the harvest
Of the mold that will one day nourish me

Every rabid raving ruse
Seduced seeds of sinking shoes
Burn through curtains
Of premature finale

Pray for death to the obvious
Shake my hand with the ominous
By tearing out every ladder rung

I have not one nail of guilt
For using the sides as stilts
Because I'm walking as high
As they tried to have me hung

Now, we all must be brave
Prepare to be chastised
We will have insane visions
While we're all skinned alive

And it's no wonder we're crazy
With fairness far away
The tightrope of our good sense
Is beginning to fray

# Disarmed

First
There was a fist
Now this
Portrayed a power
Yet also, a weakness
As the wielder's
Words did cower
The opponent
Did bewilder
Further
As his fist shot up too
But extending
His pointer finger
His middle finger
One
Two
Now, in our country this means
"PEACE!"
In another, it screams
"FUCK YOU!"
Depending on which way you face
Your feeble digits
To the fool
But this one held 'em sideways
Akin to how you hold a gun
While this was not
A weapon
He had it set
To stun

"We've gone beyond the chance of peace," he said
"And I don't exactly want to fuck you…"
She smiled
With a shy sway of her head
Disarming his whole hand
Into her
Black
And blue

# Only The Savage Survive

Stricken with loneliness
Paralytic
Chokingness
In my own home –
Where me and all my things
Allegedly belong
I walk to my lawn
In attempt
To inflate my own ego
Inept
My mind does that thing again:
"Let's think of everyone you're better than."
And I see them
The meth lab encampment
My property is ass-up against

I begin
Then end with them
Cursing myself for my shadowy prudence
These emaciated self-cannibals
Emancipated
In their own sovereign nation
Skeletal, toothless
Leave no carbon footprint
Except the one they really cookin' with
Subsisting on nothing
But ammonia, phosphorous...
Effervescence!
Harmless in the scheme of things
They just absorb the negativities
Their own heads, a bear trap
For the Devils on the peripheries

Their only worry – not to burn
The kitchen into
A blast furnace
Them and I, nearly the same
Surviving
Blasphemous!
Yet unashamed


Though still I'm jaded, unsatisfied
I follow the call
In search of calm
I drove to nowhere –


I got the sound of bombs
I know where they come from
I can see them on the horizon
These funny cities
Livestock as civilians
Simple training
Commentary
The real "savages" overseas
Somehow, our proper enemies
We'll poke the bees
Then get stung


I tried to be a good soldier once
Enduring conspiracies of her friendly fire
Just like a movie -
Her motive: my dignity
Last I heard, she was a mercenary
For hire
Where
Love
And
War
Make casualties
Intermingling

19

There it is!
That paralytic choking
From civilization's un-repentance
Is what creates
The savage: One who lives to regain their independence
The strained link of a chain
Mouth breaking open to scream its pain
But perceived as a banshee
Rebranded as one to re-tame
Or exterminate
Endgame

What a savage is not:
The instinct to build unsustainable worlds
From green fecal-stained paper which bought
Their impending collapse
A constant birth of Death
A black hole
Vacuuming
Through our minds
Our breath

The savage Earth will inherit us
As it dines on both the weak and strong
But who will be alive
Enough
To conduct
The orchestra of flies
Swarming
The dead thing
You're eating
Because you were obliged?

Only the savage will survive!

Who would assume there is dessert
The chance for love to save us?
Blood still fresh on our lips
We let slip -
"What great adversaries
We could become!"

It's all just clashing fat
Skin on skin
One on one
Between respective private parts
The gravities of two guns
Neither side
Wondering why
Or just what
We have become

With my back to the Sun
I've had enough
Only angels, on high
Could call my bluff

I kneel down to think
"Such opposition,
So high strung!"

As the universe expands
Repelling
Coming undone

A movement
An earthquake
Toothache
Pushing against dark weight

Of decay on the surface
Interpreted as violence
This inherited defiance
A true savage, cursed with this purpose

The Earth's crust slips
Trembling
As solid dirt churns
Hungry as we were
Fissures cracking
Form a path
Our humility
Finally "urned."

Then consider the graves
That we've all built upon
I am crushed by the dawn
Yet
No longer
Alone

# Paper Cuts

In rock paper scissors
The paper, near-parody

However you deploy it
The other options stay intact
While the paper gets destroyed
By its own weakness
Upon contact

Why then, from this single sheet in front of me
Do I fear for my life and mind?
Why at times would I prefer lobotomy
Than to let it find
What's behind my eyes?

It's not writer's block when you set-up barricades and armed men to
dare it to pass
Protecting your loved ones, co-workers and good citizens from your
unholy mind's wrath?

But this too, shall pass
Too much for it all to withstand
The weight of the venomous insecure rant
And what else I could do with my hands?

I shudder with that thought
The other option, though overwrought
To finally write
Never as maddening
As real life

# Patina

The muse: Courted
She said
I said
All the right words
She would later claim
She never heard

The reveal: Sordid
All of her most
Attractive traits
Armor for a life
Of self-hate

The dream: Aborted!
You can't insist
To steer a dream
When your own comet trail
Is so unclean

Her plan: Thwarted

# Slow Leak

When I was born blind
Father screamed
"Who sinned, me or the child?!?"
But he went mute, upon learning
Something anatomically wild
A heart condition
Like none
They had ever seen
The more I filled of it
The more that it leaked clean

The older I got, the more
I devoured
Everything in sight
Anything
I put in there
Was shut out
Just like the lights
An impatient hourglass
Waiting
To be smashed
Everything I thought I loved
Went right out
Just like the trash

And when I dried up every bit
Of their reserves of love
They threw rocks and insults
But that too
Was not enough
My bloody face just smiled,
"You ALL are the worst shot!
It's underneath this chest plate –
The weakest spot!"

Now, death is always knocking
But I have no time to mourn
This slow leak
In my heart
Since the day that I was born

# The Killing Tree

Yard work is the man's work
Not to mention
A fool's errand

However I tried
To quench my big oak's thirst
Its needy branches
Spring, barren

While on the next-door lot
It taunts
Another oak, blooming envy green
While that house rots
Its tree
It flaunts
Propelled by neglect
Tenants unseen

It is maddening
My hose and our tears of futility
Have poured over
Tons worth to nourish its roots
I've raked all its decay
In the same sad charade
Only to vanish
Its past power
Its proof

And then, when the sun sets just right
That other tree
The GOOD tree
Not MY tree
Throws shade on my skeletal excuse for life

But when I saw God throw down the black of eve
All the secrets revealed
The Killing Tree
At its trunk, the caches come of the coyote
Once squirrel, once bird, once cat and bunny
Now carcasses overlapping
All-natural blasphemy!
Blood dripped from the bones
Onto the fallen leaves
Seeping into circuits
Of putrid mulch, still rotting
Worms and maggots munched
Fuming pungence to feed
Screaming roots of true life
Inherent amoral need

Then I saw the whole world
As a grave upon grave
The darkness now perceived
As the subsequent shade

# Vengeance Of Spring

I made a vow
To stay in the trail
Not to trample
The new growth
But the vengeance of Spring
Made null the trail
Now beauty's blinding
Overflowth

# Warm Wind, Cold Shadow

I run
Through the soupy gusts
Of God's breath
My sweat muddies
This trail of regret
Dust gets kicked up
Like smoke from me
A goddamned rocket!

I say fuck it
I've run enough
I'm about to vomit up my guts
I keep it down
Kneel to the ground
The loudest prayer to have no sound

My eyes closed
The heat subsides
Never more glad to be alive

But what I thought to be
Absolutely
The setting sun
The cold shadow
Of the very man
I was running
From

# Prayer For Luna

As a lover of hers
And a lover of words
I immortalize her delicacy
Frequently in fetus at age forty
I pray this mirror makes transparency

She'll suffocate my every word
Claiming that "all words are empty"
Gaining might
Her parasites
The buzzards roost
On rotting prey

# Physics Revisionist

The heavier
Your heart
The faster
You sink
Into Earth

# Ex-Eternal

Since she danced into my eyes
Every sound has been music
Where once my heart didn't beat right
Now I know how to use it
As I take the reigns
Of her collapsed, deflated veins
I will ride her into the night
Our rhythm, while fleeting
Never lost its meaning
Her blood still transfuses into mine

# Birth, War, And Everyday Bleeding

Well, I've never given birth
And I've never been to war
But I beat the shit out of one of my best friends

I'll never forget his face
When he opened up the door
I made sure both his eyes got blackened

Anything not nailed down
Ended up broken on the floor
As we tangoed in a blur of ultra-violence

He just kept screaming my name
Trying to remind me who I was
While I squeezed his neck with both of my hands

The pressure made his face flush
As if the Devil could blush
But I let go because he started crying

Now to the bar to catch a buzz
The woman saw the both of us
She was so in shock, she asked us what happened

I looked my friend dead in the eye
Asking for help with my reply
I glared at her and said, "What do you think happened?"

She stood up out of her seat
And she kissed me on the cheek
And I swear to God
She started laughing

# Frozen Grin

Now, we only exist in pictures
In the ether
No anchor
Nostalgia needs the deceased
Decades
Decay
A fade
Not our long shadows
Now, demure

There once screamed a theory –
The illusion of Death
Now, our breath
Its own muted twin
The black hole in the middle of your frozen grin

I used to think we all had fangs
Now, I want to feel yours sink into my face
But you're too busy
Thinking you're too busy
Asking everybody
If you're suspended reflection was pretty
Now, it's about time
You looked into my eyes
Surprise!
Now, you must deal with me

# Fear Of Youth

I saw this coming from miles away
Have my phobias manifested
From all my past crimes up to date?
The world
All theirs to annihilate
Like it's some video game
Where nobody's got a name
Can we shove them right back up their parent's ass from which they
came?

I can't believe I'm saying this
But when I was their age
I knew a thing or two
How to channel my rage
I would hurt myself
Before I'd dream
Of hurting someone else
My fear of youth
Has got me staying inside

My buddy could not get away
When he got shot in the back
By a boy, only eighteen
My buddy died almost instantly
Blood trickled out his mouth
The boy bailed to border South
Now he'll never get to come back
To his own childhood house

The zombie apocalypse is your own child
No concept of consequence
Feral and wild
I'm afraid to see the day
When they must care for you and me
A fear of youth
Now there's nowhere to hide

Disconnected from history
They tell me to just chill out
As the whole world goes up in flames
But I need a caretaker today
To ensure this rope won't fray
Of this noose from which I sway
I've decided to let the meek
Inherit the Earth today

Being groomed to lead the massive distraction
Our youth, now every time they speak
Will read as redaction
To every daughter and son
Get the fuck off of my lawn
My fear of youth
My shotgun at my side

37

# Nice Things

I wasn't meant to have nice things
You can hear my voice crack
When I sing
The way I drop and shatter a glass
In the way I shall kick my own ass
In fact, repellant when it comes to nice things
Like an angel
Who'll singe his own wings
I've burnt holes in a $500 suit
While drinking champagne
Out of my Italian boot

And once I even had you
You were just leaving
See, I just wasn't meant
To have nice things

From the day I left my teddy bear out in the rain
To the day my ring fell right down the drain
I lost the perfect day
By stretching out a stupid night
All the way up
To the longest drop of height

And when you said you loved me
What did you mean?
Did you think it would bring
You all the nice things?

We have had and we have not
But we forgot
These are just things

Some things just scream
To be destroyed
But it's so hard
Not to avoid
These taunting things
We think define us
These haunting things
We leave behind us
We want these things
That don't know our names
Let all these things
Go up in flames

Those empty trinkets on display
Like the bride and groom
On the wedding cake
What once was you
Now is merely faked
Through all these things

# I Saw The Light

A long time ago when I was born
From that deep hole
Where shadows take flesh
And blood forms
I was awoken from the most peaceful dream
When I saw the light I kicked and screamed

I tossed
I turned
Pressed my arms out
Pushing in reverse
But they just pulled me out feet first
They could not believe
How bad I made my Mother bleed
When I saw the light I kicked and screamed

I echoed through the years
As I tried to repeat
That peaceful dream
Warm comatose sleep
Fetal position
Only me
Grabbing onto me
Denying the sun
Shining on these burning streets
But every day I must hear that alarm bell ring
And when I see the light I kick and scream

The cameras flashed on me
Molesting my mystery
The photos – overexposed
So they never really knew me

So I found dark in the drink
It took forever
Consuming countless quantity
But I always awoke
Just short of poisoning
And when I saw the light I kicked and screamed

So they made me BORN AGAIN
Cruelly
In strange meetings
From the big book
Hypocritical readings
When they mentioned Jesus
I started leaving
Yet, not without
My final warning
"I've seen the light..."

*Dedicated to Elizabeth V. Aldrich*

# Teenage Initiation

When the night spins its electric web
From the heart strings of everyone
You find yourself surrounded
Yet, unable to make a connection
You start screaming
Until you run out of breath
And that's only the first step
Of this teenage initiation

You just fall into somebody's eyes
Hypnotized
Yet untouchable as your ulcer
You can't deny the coals you must walk across
Just to get the vaguest of answer
You start crying
Until there is nothing left
Innocence and theft
In this teenage initiation

You've clenched your fists up so tight
You've punched out all of the lights
Now you're quickly dissolving
Into the night

You wanna do bad and just not be seen
But nothing works
Like it does in your wildest dreams
So instead
You just keep running
Away from or just closer to Death?
Just the other side
Of this teenage initiation

# When I Met Her In The Street

When I met her in the street
It was horizontally
I swear I saw her spirit
Escaping her body
"No, get away," she said.
"Just let me sleep."
"Let's get you up," I pled.
"Don't fall asleep,
Stay with me."

Her eyes floated up into her head like two balloons
I shook her
Stuttering
That she would feel better soon
But then she spilled her guts
She showed me all her cuts
Like ripping out a tooth
To find the truth

An ambulance
Was out of the question
The way her eyebrows raised
When I offered to call her parents
'Cause though she was a victim
They would say she had sinned
'Cause when you cross The Cross
You have crossed your kin

She finally told me her whole name
But she looked at me like it was a mistake
She couldn't recall their names
Just a white van
No windows
Unmarked plates

I carried her into our home
Keeping vigil
With a vigilante tone
Peering through blinds
For a sign
That justice might prevail

Four nameless medium-build males
God Almighty, you've failed

# Limelight Vigil

I denounce the limelight vigil
Me, bibulous
The perpetual ritual
Veiled in vapor and rancor's décor
Hands grab eager
The mist morphs to dribble
Drops fall like flies
Though still hungry to bite
Lurk
Resurrection
Like static channel hiss
'Til I find further nerve
To backhand this abyss

# The Nail That Sticks Out

Why did I go out tonight?
I gave up on my side
Of the property
I just arrived to find
Everyone, not just unkind
But playing with what they stole from me
Those who are dumb as clay
Molded into what may
Be the dirt to fall
Down the hole we dug
We cover with the rug
Of total denial

My bones stand erect
To hold my skin
A wreck
From too many nights out on the town
And I tried to seek all
The comforts of the crowd
But the nail that sticks out
Will get hammered down

I cracked the whip on the stiffs
It made no difference
At fucking all
Not one inch they moved
So my point was proved
Yet, lost on them all
And this is how we waste the day
Why people move away
Only to be bitter saps

But read these very lips
We do not slip –
We dive
Right
Through
The
Cracks

And I tried to crawl right into the sunset
But instead
Just a coffin I found
And that one crooked spike
Might have been my escape
But the nail that sticks out
Will get hammered down

# Heroine

You finally called me your hero
Baby, I'm so glad that happened
Now please, can I rescue you out of
The pretty clothes you're trapped in?

Can you tell me who else hurt you?
We'll make a list that burns as we go
As the road disappears behind the two
Of us, the horizon we overthrow

Do you need help cleaning house?
I'll wipe the floor
With any fool
Who tells us you're too young
'Cause if I don't have you
Someone else will
But I'm the best fucking one
'Cause I'll let you get away with murder
If you make my house your hideaway
You're not just my princess
You're the heiress
To this curse
Now, save my life today

*Dedicated to Alice Lou Pico*

# A Cure For Acne

The eclipsing teen
Careening to hemophilia
No one asked their permission
To inherit the hide of dinosaurs
A falsely exalted
Nostalgic continuum
Devours teen in shadow
On all fours
The curtain will not open
So they sharpen up their prop
Pointing the tool against them
"My Big Bang
Stops
Here."

# Assisted Living

From her commemorative cup
I now drink my tea
Her unopened lemon curd
I've now devoured
Like she's left no trace with me
Until, somehow
She's lying in my bed
"Grandma's not dead yet
She's just sleeping!"
Dreaming
As she's becoming
Dreams

# Discarded Arms

Take a look at these discarded arms
Too weak to strangle
To serenade or strum
Left with the taste of my own sour haste
If you think I've abused the moon
Just see what happens to the sun
When I dry those fertile fields
I make your skin easy to peel
When I condemn it as a liar
That coward ball of fire hides again

There's a black hole
Between these discarded arms
They stole the work from God
The fires and the flood
But now their work is done
And they're waiting for you, dear
To hold you now
Oblivious
In blissful ignorance
To the beating death drums
Echoing on and on

And as night falls like an anvil to our heads
I will not rest
Until it swallows up the West
We are two bitter pills
That could never be refilled
But the night is holding me under its tongue

# Acknowledgments

Special thanks to Craig Douglas, Stephen J. Golds, Kev, and Chris at Close To The Bone and to all in the First Cut Poetry Collective.

# Gabriel Hart

Gabriel Hart lives in Morongo Valley in California's High Desert. His Palm Springs noir novelette *A Return To Spring* is out now Mannison Press. He's also the author of the dispo-pocalyptic twin-novel *Virgins In Reverse / The Intrusion* (Traveling Shoes Press) which contains a foreword by avant-rockabilly provocateur Tav Falco. Other works have appeared in *Pulp Modern, Shotgun Honey, ExPat Press, Bristol Noir, Close To The Bone, Black Hare Press,* and *Crime Poetry Weekly.* He is a regular contributor to *Lit Reactor, EconoClash Review,* Space Cowboy's *Simultaneous Times* podcast, as well as *L.A. Record,* a Los Angeles underground music publication. Hart also taught the writing workshop for Mil-Tree, a non-profit reach out program for Vets and Active Duty Military to heal the wounds of war.

His musical alter-ego sees him as the ringleader of the L.A. based punk Wall of Sound group Jail Weddings, who released their third album *Wilted Eden* in 2019. Their previous album *Meltdown: A Declaration of Unpopular Emotion* (2013) was voted Best Album of The Year by L.A. Weekly, followed by Best Band of the Year in 2014.